MANAGING TEAMS

ROBERT HELLER

DORLING KINDERSLEY

London • New York • Sydney • Moscow

A DORLING KINDERSLEY BOOK

Project Editor Sasha Heseltine
Project Art Editor Darren Hill
Editor Marian Broderick
Designer Austin Barlow

DTP Designer Jason Little
Production Controllers Silvia La Greca,
Michelle Thomas

Series Editor Jane Simmonds
Series Art Editor Tracy Hambleton-Miles

Managing Editor Stephanie Jackson
Managing Art Editor Nigel Duffield

First published in Great Britain in 1998
by Dorling Kindersley Limited,
9 Henrietta Street,
London WC2E 8PS

A CIP catalogue record for this book is available
from the British Library

ISBN 0 7513 0628 2

Reproduced by Colourscan, Singapore
Printed and bound in Italy by Graphicom srl

CONTENTS

WORKING FOR THE FUTURE

IMPROVING TEAM EFFICIENCY

INTRODUCTION

Working with teams, whether as leader of a single team or manager of several, is an essential part of a manager's remit. Teamworking is rapidly becoming the preferred practice in many organizations as traditional corporate hierarchies give way to flat, multi-skilled working methods. Managing Teams is an indispensable and practical guide to leading teams with expertise, covering subjects such as defining the skills required to complete a project, establishing trust between individuals within a team, and maximizing the performance of that team. This book is vital reading for anyone involved in teamwork, whether as a novice or as an experienced team leader. A self-assessment exercise allows you to assess your own leadership abilities and potential, and 101 concise tips offer practical advice.

UNDERSTANDING HOW TEAMS WORK

Teamwork is the foundation of all successful management. Managing teams well is a major and stimulating challenge to any manager, from novice to experienced hand.

WHAT MAKES A GOOD TEAM?

A true team is a living, constantly changing, dynamic force in which a number of people come together to work. Team members discuss their objectives, assess ideas, make decisions, and work towards their targets together.

Team member has idea prompted by presentation

Team leader assesses new idea

WORKING TOGETHER

All successful teams demonstrate the same fundamental features: strong and effective leadership; the establishment of precise objectives; making informed decisions; the ability to act quickly upon these decisions; communicating freely; mastering the requisite skills and techniques to fulfil the project in hand; providing clear targets for the team to work towards; and – above all – finding the right balance of people prepared to work together for the common good of the team.

I Remember that each member has something to add to your team.

ANALYZING TEAM TASKS

Successful teams can be formed by 2 to 25 or more people, but much more important than size is shape – the pattern of working into which team members settle to perform their given tasks. There are three basic methods of performing a task:

● Repetitive tasks and familiar work require each team member to have a fixed role, which is fulfilled independently, as on assembly lines;

● Projects that require some creative input require team members to have fixed roles and working procedures, but also to work in unison, as when generating new products;

2 Formulate team objectives carefully, and always take them seriously.

● Work that demands constant creative input and personal contributions requires people to work very closely as partners. This style of working is prevalent among senior management.

Colleague introduces new idea to group

Listener watches reactions of team before delivering opinion

One member of team questions all new ideas

◀ **WORKING WELL TOGETHER**
A team of managers discusses a new plan that has been put forward by a member of the team. All of the team members are free to join the discussion. Later, the team leader will assess the contributions.

ACHIEVING POTENTIAL

There is no limit to the potential of a good team. Given an "impossible" task, team members will reinforce each other's confidence as they seek to turn the "impossible" into reality. The collective ability to innovate is stronger than that of the individual because the combined brainpower of a team, however small in number, exceeds that of any one person. By harnessing this power, a team can go beyond simple, useful improvements to achieve real breakthroughs. For example, in one company an engineering team was asked to double machine reliability. They thought it impossible, but went on to produce a plan that trebled performance.

3 Remember that team members must support each other.

4 Break long-term aims into short-term projects.

WORKING COLLECTIVELY

To harness and take full advantage of team-power, the individual brains and personalities involved must be encouraged to collaborate. This process is vital in generating results. Giving stretching goals to a team will encourage it to work collectively and introduce a sense of urgency – potentially eliminating bureaucracy as it concentrates on getting positive results in the shortest possible time. The impact of a single team breakthrough can, by its example, galvanize an entire company.

▼ **WORKING TOWARDS UNDERSTANDING**
Encouraging open communication and the free flow of information within a team ensures that each member is fully aware of the talents and experience available within the group.

KNOWING TEAM GOALS

Once a team has been formed, the next major step is to establish its goals. There is little point in having a team that is raring to go if its members are all pursuing disparate aims. Goals may well change over the course of a team's existence; for example, if a new product is being launched on to the market, the first priority will be for the team to concentrate on research into its competition. If the aim is to improve customer satisfaction, the first goal will be to find ways of providing a higher standard of service. According to the circumstance, teamworking goals might include:

- Increasing the rate of productivity in a manufacturing company;
- Improving the quality of production;
- Involving all employees in the decision-making process to increase job satisfaction;
- Looking at working systems and practices to reduce time wastage;
- Working together with customers to build closer relationships so that the needs of the market can be better understood.

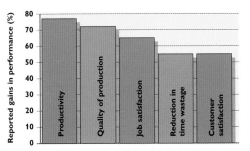

| 5 | Allocate a clear deadline for each of your projects. |

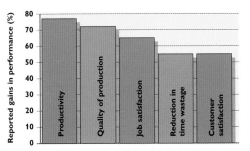

▲ IMPROVING PERFORMANCE

In a survey of 230 personnel executives, the American Society of Training and Development found that teamworking led to a substantial rise in performance in key areas.

CULTURAL DIFFERENCES

Cross-functional, multi-disciplinary, interdepartmental teams are spreading fast in the West, having been established in Japan for many years. In some British companies, managers already spend half their time working in such teams; and the democratic attitudes of many North Americans have helped them to adapt well to this way of working. Continental Europeans still tend to be more comfortable with the traditional hierarchical systems, but increasing competitive pressures and the need for speed-to-market are now forcing change on managers in many industries.

MATCHING TEAM TO TASK

There are numerous types of team, formal and informal, each suited to fulfilling particular tasks. Team leaders need to understand the objectives and goals of their team clearly in order to match tasks to the most appropriate style of team.

6 Decide early on what style of team is appropriate for your objectives.

7 Try to form strong bonds with other team members of formal or informal teams.

FORMAL TEAMS

Formal teams are fundamental to an organization – whether internal audit units or counter-staff in a supermarket. They are often permanent, carry out repetitive work, and have a defined remit:

- Cross-functional executive teams exist at director level to pool high levels of expertise;
- Cross-functional teams at all levels pool their knowledge to solve problems and run projects;
- Business teams at all levels of an organization place people with similar expertise in long-term teams to oversee specific projects;
- Formal support teams provide internal expert administration back-up in their own fields.

INFORMAL TEAMS

Casual groupings of people come together to work on an informal basis throughout all organizations. Informal teams can be formed on an *ad hoc* basis to deal with many needs:

- Temporary project teams stay together for the duration of a specific task;
- Change teams discuss strategy or trouble-shoot when a particular, one-off problem occurs;
- "Hot groups" brainstorm creative projects while retaining autonomy and spontaneity;
- Temporary task forces deal informally with specific short-term tasks and issues.

8 Find a sponsor – a senior individual who can promote the team's work.

9 Remind members that they are all team participants.

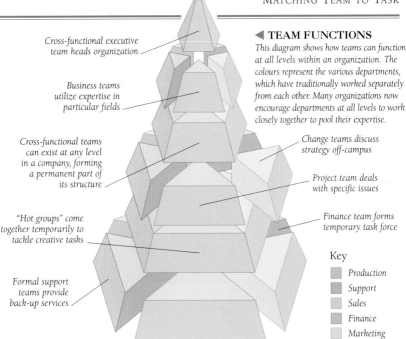

◀ **TEAM FUNCTIONS**
This diagram shows how teams can function at all levels within an organization. The colours represent the various departments, which have traditionally worked separately from each other. Many organizations now encourage departments at all levels to work closely together to pool their expertise.

Cross-functional executive team heads organization

Business teams utilize expertise in particular fields

Cross-functional teams can exist at any level in a company, forming a permanent part of its structure

"Hot groups" come together temporarily to tackle creative tasks

Formal support teams provide back-up services

Change teams discuss strategy off-campus

Project team deals with specific issues

Finance team forms temporary task force

Key
- Production
- Support
- Sales
- Finance
- Marketing

COMPARING FORMAL AND INFORMAL TEAMS

The more formal the team, the more disciplined its leadership tends to be: company rules and procedures have to be followed, reports made, progress noted, and results obtained on a regular basis. By the same token, informal teams follow informal procedures. Ideas and solutions to problems can be generated on a more casual basis and procedures are less stringent. However, it is important to remember that team leadership always has to be results-oriented, whether in a formal or informal team. For example, the temporary, casual nature of a "hot group" brainstorming a project should not be an excuse to do away with team discipline altogether.

POINTS TO REMEMBER

- A team member is still an individual, and should always be treated as such.
- Cross-functional teams offer people the chance to learn about the roles and work of others.
- Inter-departmental teams break down costly barriers.
- Formal teams sometimes need informal elements to stimulate and refresh their work.
- Teams cease to be teams if one member becomes dominant.
- All team members should make sure that they are working towards the same goals.

CHOOSING TEAM MEMBERS

One of the secrets of successful team leadership is matching the skills of team members carefully to the type of task they are required to perform. For example, if a product launch requires the generation of new ideas, a team should be cross-functional, comprising people from different disciplines who can apply their varied expertise and creativity to study a project from several different angles. If, however, a task requires specialist knowledge of accounting procedures, it makes sense to recruit specifically among the leading minds of a financial division. As the demands of a project change, it may be necessary to introduce different talents into a team and replace members whose roles are no longer relevant.

10 Fix goals that are measurable to keep your team focused.

11 Make use of the great power of friendship to strengthen a team.

BUILDING ON FRIENDSHIPS WITHIN A TEAM

It is important to generate an easy, friendly atmosphere in a formal team meeting, even though the imposition of official procedures contrasts with the casual, occasionally even disorderly tone of an unofficial or informal team meeting. Try to create an atmosphere in which all ideas get a respectful hearing and conversation is open. This is easier if team members can relate to each other as people rather than simply as colleagues, so encourage members of both formal and informal teams to spend time together outside their official meetings. Arrange social events and celebrate a team's successes to help maintain a friendly atmosphere. Encourage people to spend time together out of work hours – genuine friendships between individuals have a unifying effect on a team as a whole.

◀ **TALKING INFORMALLY**
Talking to colleagues outside office hours or in an informal environment helps build up a bond within the team. Encourage informal gatherings as good opportunities to exchange views and opinions in a relaxed atmosphere.

MATCHING TYPES OF TEAM TO CERTAIN TASKS

TYPES OF TEAM	TASKS AND CHARACTERISTICS
EXECUTIVE TEAM A cross-functional group headed by chief executive. Members chosen by role, for example, finance director.	● Manages organization or divisional operation on day-to-day basis. Meets regularly, with agenda and minutes. ● Depends on information from lower levels. If badly controlled, can be forum for personality battles.
CROSS-FUNCTIONAL TEAM A multi-disciplinary, inter-departmental team, found at any level in an organization.	● Removes obstacles to exchange of ideas in a variety of specific tasks – for example, a new product launch. ● Team members bring their different areas of expertise and skill to a problem or task.
BUSINESS TEAM A group of people in charge of the long-term running of a project or unit within their organization.	● Runs a unit and optimizes its results. ● Depends on the leader, who may change too often for the group to settle into optimal team-working. Usually subject to fairly close supervision.
FORMAL SUPPORT TEAM A team providing support and services, such as finance, information systems, administration, and staffing.	● Carries heavy load of routine work, such as the postal system, whose efficiency is indispensable for success. ● Depends on processes, offering scope for raising productivity by teamwork. Tends to be clannish.
PROJECT TEAM A team selected and kept together for the duration of a project, such as the construction of a new facility.	● Requires a large number of sub-groups, sub-tasks, and detailed planning, plus tight discipline. ● Depends on close understanding among members and well-organized work practices.
CHANGE TEAM A group of experts briefed to achieve change. Value depends on collective ability. Sometimes starts off-campus.	● Influences corporate cultures to achieve radical improvement in results by applying new methods. ● Led by believers in change, with a high level of dedication to their organization.
HOT GROUP An autonomous body set apart from the rest of an organization, often in a remote site.	● Concentrates on tasks such as moving into new markets or creating new product programmes. ● Flexible, independent, and high-achieving groups of people who question assumptions and get fast results.
TEMPORARY TASK FORCE A short-term body set up to study or solve a specific problem or issue and report back to management.	● Establishes new IT systems, removes production bottlenecks, or involves itself in similar tasks, usually working under intense time pressures. ● Uses informal processes and generates alternatives.

Analyzing Team Roles

In an effective team, each member knows their role thoroughly. While having their own strengths, skills, and roles, they must also contribute to the "togetherness" of the team. It is the role of either team leader or senior manager to see that this happens.

Assessing Leadership Qualities

All leaders need strong personality traits to assert influence and function. Some of these attributes are internal, such as vision, but they always have to be complemented by external qualities, such as high visibility, to produce the utmost from team members. A team leader needs to be both facilitator and inspirer – a business team depends upon its leader to provide it with the facility to make decisions and the support to grow.

12 Always choose leaders on merit, regardless of other considerations.

13 Look for a strong team commitment from a leader.

▼ **EVALUATING LEADERSHIP QUALITIES**
The analysis of leadership qualities shown below was developed by the UK's Insights consultancy and is influenced heavily by the example of famous sports stars. The model indicates the five internal and five external skills that should be present in a successful leader of teams.

Key
☐ *Inner strengths*
☐ *Outer signs*

Communication

Vision

Self-belief

Commitment

Visibility

Results-focused

Integrity

Attentiveness

Courage

Teamwork

LEADING A TEAM

The performance of any team depends on the quality of its collective thinking. How good are its decisions? This reflects the quality of the decision-making processes. The leader should strive to achieve a positive atmosphere, free from rigidity and envy, in which people compete with ideas – not egos. Teamwork does not function if the leader consistently puts forward ideas before others have had the chance to speak. In the classic Japanese method, the leader listens silently until every team member has expressed an opinion before making the decision for the whole team. A true team leader will facilitate, inspire, and implement rather than control.

 14 Always reward merit, but never let errors go unremarked.

▼ **GIVING INSPIRATION**
Team leaders play several roles: they are there to facilitate the making of decisions, inspire lateral thinking, motivation, and hard work within the team, and to implement decisions made by the team.

Facilitate ➡ **Inspire** ➡ **Implement**

UNDERSTANDING LEADERSHIP FUNCTIONS

The main task and function of a leader is to achieve the goals of the team. If you are team leader, ensure that team goals are achieved via these processes:

- Planning roles to be filled and selecting appropriate individuals;
- Leading the team in meetings, starting with a discussion of team objectives and values;
- Ensuring that targets are met and that values – above all, the values of working collectively – are observed by the team;
- Analyzing and correcting failures swiftly and surely – but always remembering to celebrate the successes just as enthusiastically;
- Carrying the responsibility of representing the team loyally to others, both inside and outside the organization.

CULTURAL DIFFERENCES

Styles of leadership vary internationally. British managers often conceal firm orders behind apparently woolly statements, while German leaders invite the views of their teams, but retain control of all decision-making. Americans are accustomed to blunt, assertive leadership, and the Japanese to a consensus, in which unanimous agreement is reached through a laborious process. True teamwork may bring these styles closer together.

CONSIDERING ROLES

For a team to function most efficiently there are several key roles that should be filled. These include co-ordinator, ideas person, critic, external contact, implementer, team leader, and inspector. It is useful to bear these roles in mind when you are considering candidates for team membership, although you should also look for people with the ability to perform the specific tasks on which your team's operations depend. Never forget that the most important function of a team is to achieve the objective of the task in hand. Remember, too, that a friendly and open personality, and the ability and willingness to work with a group of people, are indispensable characteristics for a team player.

DIVIDING UP ROLES

It does not make sense to fit people into a strait-jacket. You may find a perfectly equipped external contact or critic, you may not. Try to match roles to personality rather than attempting to shoehorn the personality into the role. It is not necessary for each person to perform only one function. If the team has only a small number of members, doubling or trebling up the roles is fine – as long as all the needs of the team are truly covered and the members feel comfortable with their roles.

15 Remember that everyone in a team thinks in a different way.

Implementer also acts as team critic

Ideas person also deals with external contacts

Team leader also takes on roles of co-ordinator and inspector

◀ **SMALLER TEAMS**
Double or treble up roles when a team has only a few members, to ensure that all the key requirements for the successful completion of the task are catered for.

IDENTIFYING THE KEY ROLES WITHIN TEAMS

TEAM ROLES

CHARACTERISTICS

TEAM LEADER
Finds new team members and develops the teamworking spirit.

- Excellent judge of the talents and personalities of individuals within the team.
- Adept at finding ways of overcoming weaknesses.
- Is a first-class two-way communicator.
- Good at inspiring and sustaining enthusiasm.

CRITIC
Guardian and analyst of the team's long-term effectiveness.

- Never satisfied with less than the best solution.
- Expert at analyzing solutions to find the possible weaknesses within them.
- Merciless in insisting that faults be corrected.
- Constructive in pointing way to possible remedies.

IMPLEMENTER
Ensures the momentum and smooth-running of the team's actions.

- A born time-tabler who thinks methodically.
- Anticipates threatening delays in schedule in time for them to be prevented.
- Has a "can-do" mentality and loves to fix things.
- Able to rally support and overcome defeatism.

EXTERNAL CONTACT
Looks after the team's external relationships.

- Diplomatic, and good judge of the needs of others.
- Has a reassuring, authoritative presence.
- Has an effective grasp of the overall picture of the team's work.
- Discreet when handling confidential information.

CO-ORDINATOR
Pulls together the work of the team as a whole into a cohesive plan.

- Understands how difficult tasks inter-relate.
- Has a strong sense of priorities
- Has a mind able to grasp several things at once.
- Good at maintaining internal contacts.
- Skilled at heading off potential trouble.

IDEAS PERSON
Sustains and encourages the team's innovative vitality and energy.

- Enthusiastic and lively, with a zest for new ideas.
- Eager for and receptive to the ideas of others.
- Sees problems as opportunities for successful innovation, rather than as disasters.
- Never at a loss for a hopeful suggestion.

INSPECTOR
Ensures that high standards are sought and maintained.

- Strict, and sometimes even pedantic in enforcing rigorous standards within the team.
- Good judge of the performance of other people.
- Unhesitating in bringing problems to the surface.
- Able to praise as well as to find fault.

BALANCING SKILLS WITHIN A TEAM

Acquiring the right mix of experience in a team can be more difficult than finding the basic skills, but is vital if the team is to be effective. Encourage each team member to make their own individual contribution, both on a technical and a personal level.

16 When recruiting people for a team, look for their growth potential.

17 Pay close attention to lack of relevant experience in group members.

FINDING THE RIGHT BALANCE OF SKILLS

Look for team members who possess one of the three major types of skill, that are vital for the success of a team's task. These are:

- Technical expertise in disciplines (such as engineering and marketing);
- Problem-solving skills and the ability to make clear, informed decisions;
- Teamworking skills and an ability to cope well with interpersonal relationships.

MAINTAINING THE RIGHT BALANCE OF SKILLS

As a project proceeds, the range of skills needed within the team can change. For example, some specialist skills that were vital at the outset of a team's life may become superfluous as the project develops. To maintain the right balance of complementary skills, a team leader must be able to recognize any changes in project or team needs and act accordingly. This ability is as important in team leaders as their ability to evaluate the technical and analytical skills of potential team members. Both individuals and team need the power to grow.

18 Take people out of the team if they do not perform.

19 Find people with a good level of personal skill, and help develop them.

CHOOSING INDIVIDUALS FOR SPECIFIC ROLES

DO'S

DON'TS

Draw up a job profile before starting to talk to people

Which qualities are required for the role?

Assume that anyone will suit the role within the team

Check "on paper" profile against details of individuals

Are there any suitable people?

Rely solely on word-of-mouth recommendations

Favour individuals with wide-ranging skills

What are their respective key strengths?

Ignore shortfalls in favour of particular experience

Give serious consideration to any shortcomings

Can any weakness be overcome?

Hope weaknesses will be overlooked by the team

Note any shortcomings in personal skills

Will I enjoy working with this person?

Ignore signs of individual not being a team player

Expect them to overcome problems "on the job"

Offer the role to the individual who brings most overall to the team

Make a final decision based on responses to the questions above

Offer the role to the individual who excels at one particular skill

SETTING UP
A TEAM

Establishing a team is the leader's prime task. Make sure your team has a clear purpose and sufficient resources to achieve it. Be open and impartial in your treatment of team members.

SETTING GOALS

What is your team for? The question may sound obvious, but time spent at the beginning of a project in defining team objectives is crucial to a successful outcome. Make sure that you have clearly established the issues that the team needs to resolve.

20 Set challenging goals that are still realistic in view of your deadlines.

POINTS TO REMEMBER

- All team members need to agree on a precise definition of what they are working towards.
- Goals should not be set until you have discussed all possible approaches to the task.
- Although team members are needed to finalize team goals, the objectives of the team can also dictate membership.
- For best results targets should be challenging, with a combination of general and specific goals.

BUILDING A CONSENSUS

Meetings are an excellent way of fostering team spirit and the team-working habit in the early stages of a team's existence. Set up an initial series of meetings in which members can get to know each other and work towards a consensus about the goals of the team. Make sure that the task the team has been assigned and the issues it will be addressing are fully understood by everyone, and assess all the options available to the team before deciding how the team will be organized. Finally, discuss and decide on achievable deadlines for all the elements of the project.

ANALYZING GOALS

Goals will vary according to whether a team is there to recommend a course of action, to make or do something, or to run something. For example, a task force that makes a recommendation can measure its success rates against feedback from within the organization. A "doing" or "making" team, such as a manufacturing cell, has specific costs and customer satisfaction targets to work towards. A team charged with running a marketing drive has to work to strict budgets and schedules.

> **21** Consider the aims of individual team members when setting targets.

HARNESSING MOTIVATION

Ambitious, challenging goals are more motivational than smaller, specific ones. For example, aiming to be biggest and best in retail financial services is more motivational than trying to reduce average mortgage application approval to two days. If possible, set both general *and* specific goals, aiming high but remaining realistic. Ensure that everybody participates in setting their own goals, as well as the team's. Do not compromise on any teamwork needs. Look for the optimum combination of strong teamwork and technical capabilities.

> **22** Do not let failure of one part of a project jeopardize its overall success.

▼ **TAKING AN OVERVIEW**
Take into account all the aspects of your appointed task or project, and discuss them with team members when defining the team's overall goals.

Timescale
Work out realistic deadlines for the team to complete its task

Constraints
Assess how much autonomy the team has, and its limitations

Priorities
Assess the order in which key elements in the project must be completed

Sub-goals
Break down targets and budgets for sub-groups and individuals

Vision
Set out attainable, but demanding, long-term goals

Budget
Prepare the budget, allowing for staff salaries and any additional resources

PROVIDING SUPPORT FOR A TEAM

A degree of independence is essential in successful teamwork, but few teams are able to stand completely alone. Nurture good relations and support systems within your organization that satisfy both your team's needs and corporate requirements.

23 Insist on having IT support that gives you exactly what you want.

PROVIDING BASIC SUPPORT

Most teams are supported by the technical and administrative infrastructure of the organization to which they belong. It often makes little sense to set up an accounting system within a team, especially as external financial control can help to limit financial outlay. However, there are some exceptions, notably in information systems: the danger of relying on a centralized IT department is that your team will not receive the specific software support that it requires in order to complete a particular task successfully. To overcome this difficulty, some teams incorporate their own IT expertise. Think carefully about any specialist support your team is likely to need, and then discuss the options for acquiring it with all the team members.

PROVIDING SUPPORT FROM WITHIN AN ORGANIZATION

Sales staff offer information on markets and contacts

Administrative help provides vital back-up to the project

The accounts department provides financial expertise

Senior staff members are available to make decisions

Specialized help is called in when required

THE TEAM, with vital support in place, operates at peak efficiency

Setting Up Links with Management

All teams need to have the backing of the senior staff in the parent organization. The three key relationships a team needs are: the main team sponsor, the head of the department or operation to which the team reports, and whoever controls the team's budget. Their roles are to monitor and approve the team's activities, and to ensure that all necessary practical support is available. Keep strong lines of communication going with these managers – this becomes even more important if your team is based away from headquarters, for example, in a factory or separate office building.

24 Treat external consultants as team members.

25 Keep your team sponsor informed of progress.

Choosing a Location for a Team

Location	Implications	Example
Head Office Team occupies space in company headquarters, near other related activities, with managers in separate offices.	● Close to management to liaise with decision-makers. ● May be separate from main production source and thus some internal customers.	A group responsible for organizing distribution, working on plans for centralizing warehouses in a location overseas.
Factory Team is part of operational unit or attached to regional or local office: managers are on same site.	● Physical closeness to manufacturing is helpful. ● Distance from headquarters and decision-makers can cause delays or problems.	Specialist marketing group for products made on site, with managers reporting back to marketing director at company headquarters.
"Skunk Works" Special project team occupies make-do premises remote from other corporate activities. Management on site.	● Facilitates very high level of group dedication, team spirit, and teamwork. ● Can lose support, lack realism, or become isolated.	New product or business development where corporate mould needs to be broken, so that physical and managerial separation is vital.
"Ivory Tower" Long-term project team is set apart from the rest of the organization in permanent offices. Management on site.	● Suits professional operation run to high standards. ● Remoteness from internal customers and market may promote arrogance.	Information systems team, responsible for planning, purchasing, maintaining, and controlling computer-based activities on all company sites.

ESTABLISHING TEAM TRUST

The most essential feature of successful teamwork is trust. Teams thrive on mutual trust, so it must be established early in the life of a team. Promote mutual trust through delegation, openness of conduct and communication, and a free exchange of ideas.

26 Keep tasks to yourself only if you know that no-one else can do them.

27 Do not delegate any unnecessary work – scrap it.

28 Give your team the freedom to make its own decisions.

LEARNING TO DELEGATE

Delegation takes two forms: delegation of tasks and of authority. Teamwork needs both for mutual trust to develop. Break down each project into single tasks or goals, and allocate them to individual team members. Then leave well alone, intervening only if it appears that a goal will not be achieved. To delegate authority, share your power both with the team, consulting members on all issues, and with individuals, giving them full authority if their area of expertise is involved. Ask members to keep you informed of progress – and let them get on with it.

RECOGNIZING CHARACTER TYPES WHEN DELEGATING

CAN DO – WILL DO
The ideal delegate, happy to accept full responsibility for his specific task and also happy to consult others, acting on the advice that is given.

WILL DO – CAN'T DO
Initially the delegate may require encouragement and proper training to overcome inexperience before taking responsibility for the allotted task.

CAN DO – WON'T DO
A reluctance to learn or accept other opinions may mean that an individual is simply not a team-player, and therefore not a strong delegate.

CAN'T DO – WON'T DO
Unless this person's lack of motivation and ability can be overcome, delegation will fail, and he may have to be moved to another environment.

PROMOTING OPENNESS

Teamwork and secrecy cannot live together, so a leader who is not open with team members will not get the best of their potential. Arrange regular formal and informal meetings to serve as avenues to openness. As people get to know one another better, they will relax and start to feel at ease with the team – and this will allow a sense of loyalty and cohesion to develop. Try to allow the team full access (where appropriate) to all facts and figures, agendas, and minutes relevant to their overall responsibilities for the project, but bear in mind that there will be times when you may have to maintain confidentiality.

CULTURAL DIFFERENCES

Attitudes towards teamworking vary around the world. Members of British teams may be inhibited about expressing themselves in front of others until a rapport has been established. A North American team is unlikely to have any such qualms, and may bounce ideas off each other from the time of their first meeting.

29 Encourage positive contributions from team members.

ENCOURAGING IDEAS

People have far more potential for creating ideas when working as a team than they do individually. Encourage the open discussion of ideas, and make sure that all suggestions are heard with respect. If an idea needs to be discounted, do so with tact, and always give valid reasons for the rejection. Alert team members to the expertise available within the group, and always promote the open discussion of ideas relevant to the objectives.

CREATING ▼ NEW IDEAS
When holding a creative session, ask attendees to come with two or three prepared ideas to present to colleagues.

Record all ideas and evaluate them afterwards

Maximizing Performance

It is vital that all members of a team work together to maximize team performance. Give people full responsibility for their jobs and empower them to execute and improve their own work in ways that optimize their contribution to the entire team.

30 Acknowledge, publicize, and celebrate all team successes.

Awarding Responsibility

The first duty of any person working in a team is to attend to their own job. To make a team work together successfully, however, responsibility must go beyond the individual. Award your team total responsibility for achieving its own goals. Create a sense of responsibility in each individual so that they are happy to fulfil their allotted tasks to the best of their ability. Do this by delegating tasks efficiently and monitoring each team member's performance, as well as that of the team as a whole. In this way you will promote the sharing of responsibility among team members, and encourage individuals to assist their colleagues and enhance the overall performance of the team.

Points to Remember

- Each team member should be able to cover the role of at least one other member.
- People should be given the responsibility to act on their own initiative within a team.
- A large task will be better handled if the entire project is handed over to a team.
- People need to be aware of where their own responsibilities begin and end.
- Each team member needs to be encouraged to find their own best method of working.

31 Find an easily accessible way of displaying team progress daily.

Sharing Responsibility

Drawing up common aims and agreeing individual roles when a team is set up is only the beginning of a process that has to last as long as the team does. A team must be responsible for implementing their policies, monitoring progress, and responding creatively and constructively where action is falling short of objectives. It is also the responsibility of the team as a whole to ensure that there is a free flow of communication among members – everybody needs to be kept fully informed about progress and changes in policy.

ENSURING PEAK PERFORMANCE

As team leader, your role is to facilitate your team's efficiency. You can do this by taking responsibility for a number of different functions:

- Ensuring that all the members of your team are aware of their responsibilities and are challenged by their work;
- Encouraging team members to contribute their best to both the team and the task in hand;
- Overseeing the team's work practices to ensure that individual members work towards a common end;
- Assessing and setting team goals at the correct level to inspire continued motivation;
- Making sure that any overlap between team and individual responsibilities does not result in duplicated tasks.

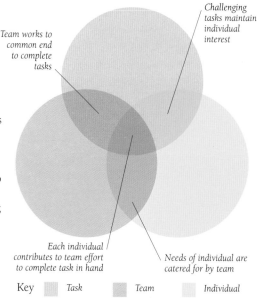

Challenging tasks maintain individual interest

Team works to common end to complete tasks

Each individual contributes to team effort to complete task in hand

Needs of individual are catered for by team

Key | Task | Team | Individual

▲ UNIFYING A TEAM

Most teams have a tendency to place too much focus on the task and not enough on the individual. This model shows an ideal situation in which the needs of the individual, the dynamics of the group, and the requirements of the task coincide at four strategic points to produce a unified, effective working team.

---

32 Encourage people to form working partnerships within the team.

BEING FLEXIBLE

Any team demands much of its members. While each member of the team has their own role and responsibility, they should remain flexible and willing to adapt to change. Some manufacturing groups require members to be able to fulfil every aspect of their team's work. Show flexibility by sharing aspects of your leadership role, and help team members by providing an assistant to share or take over some of their duties. As the team develops and progresses, look at individual roles, and modify them as and when the task requires it.

CREATING A SELF-MANAGED TEAM

Self-managed teams (SMTs) are more independent than other teams. They are found increasingly in organizations that have flattened their structures and cut out layers of middle-management and supervisory levels as they reform their working practices.

33 Encourage natural leaders to lead and develop their leadership skills.

DEFINING SMTS

34 Never reject a team idea without explaining why, frankly and fully.

Self-managed teams take on total responsibility for a specific project from inception to conclusion – for example, a manufacturing cell might take over the entire production process from an assembly line. Characteristics of these teams include the sharing of leadership roles, a high rate of autonomy, open discussion leading to democratic decision-making, control over team activities, and total self-accountability, which is based on individual and team results.

REAPING THE BENEFITS

When running properly, a self-managed team can be very productive. It can save on management costs, raise levels of quality and customer service, cut out process steps, reduce waste, and introduce more flexibility in the workplace. In addition to the economic benefits, such a team can provide a daily training ground for its members, who may need to develop their skills to take on the responsibilities of self-management. If the system works, expect to see a rise in employee morale and retention, and, with experience, more ability to react swiftly to changes in the marketplace.

35 Make sure that the team keeps in contact with its customers.

▲ RUNNING AN SMT
Allow a self-managed team to take full responsibility for its own actions. Give guidance only when it is specifically requested – so that members will be free to gain new experience and skills.

POINTS TO REMEMBER

- Teams usually respond well to having autonomy in all matters.
- SMTs should be responsible for setting their own high targets.
- Teamwork should focus on customer satisfaction.
- Consistent quality needs to be maintained at all times.
- The team should be able to ask for outside help when it is needed – but only then.

SUPPORTING SMTs

To work effectively, self-managed teams need full backing and support from a management that appreciates their need for autonomy. This means allowing team members a full say in any decision that affects them, including pay, performance measures, and personnel matters. Although a nominal team leader may be installed by senior management, that leader's position will be entirely dependent upon the consent of the others in the team. Aspects of leadership can change: a new talent may come to the fore, or the project may change direction. One of the more difficult aspects of working with SMTs is psychological: managers are required to surrender a major part of their right to manage the SMT while still monitoring its progress. Be flexible enough to accept that good decisions may be taken without you.

TAKING ON AN EXISTING TEAM

Taking on an established team is a testing experience. While you share the learning process with a team in a start-up situation, a takeover demands immediate evidence of your ability to take charge and recognize team strengths.

36 Show your team who is in charge by being assertive, but not aggressive.

BECOMING A TEAM LEADER

When a new leader joins an existing team, caution and doubt co-exist with hope and interest on both sides. Try to make a favourable, positive first impression. Much may depend on the previous leader's standing and the cause of the change. If the team you have inherited has done well under good, strong leadership, recognize that – if not, presume that the members hunger for reform. Even if your predecessor was disliked and regarded as incompetent, or if the team is failing, never dwell negatively on past faults or poor performance. Demonstrate trust, promote team togetherness, and appear quietly confident. Insist on producing a competitive performance, achieved with the full support of your new team.

New leader's body language is open

▲ MEETING FOR THE FIRST TIME
When meeting a new team, be relaxed and confident without appearing arrogant. Keep your body language open and friendly so that you look both approachable and natural.

37 Think of ways to make an instant good impression on a new team – but without being over-eager.

TALKING TO A NEW TEAM

Find out about your new team's background, purpose, progress, and membership before you meet them. Other people's input can be valuable at this stage, but trust your own judgment as you start to form an opinion of the team's abilities. Remember that your best chance to observe the team will come only once you have taken charge. Soon after taking on the team, set aside time to talk to each member, one-to-one, about their individual tasks and the project as a whole, their views of their own performance, whether they favour any changes in working practice, and, if so, why. From their ideas, you will gain a clear insight into each individual's character, motivation, and abilities. Avoid asking individuals to assess their colleagues – it is up to you to form your own opinion.

THINGS TO DO

1. Socialize with the team as often as you can to know people better and become better known yourself.

2. Show you appreciate the skills of the team to prevent any resentment.

3. Actively show your willingness to listen to team members.

4. Show your authority from the outset with confidence – otherwise you may find yourself being undermined.

BECOMING A TEAM MEMBER

The rules of being new to a team are simple. Form a clear idea of your personal goals, and work towards fitting them to the purposes of the team. If there is anybody you know already in the team, use them to ease your way into the group. Strive to make a good impression, but do not appear to be over-confident. Observe the culture of the team, and once you are comfortable with what you have learned about your colleagues and your new task, begin to show your own capabilities and initiative.

38 If you ask people for their advice, be prepared not only to welcome it, but also to act on it.

INTRODUCING A NEW TEAM MEMBER

When old team members are replaced by new staff, encourage and welcome the opportunity for new ideas and approaches, rather than expecting them to follow previous ways of working. Never just leave new members to make their own introductions and find their own way around the team: instead, ensure that each new member has a "minder" to pilot them through their early weeks. At the first opportunity, for instance at a team meeting, introduce new members to the group and ask the newcomers to say a few words about themselves – but prepare them beforehand.

IMPROVING TEAM EFFICIENCY

Teams are properly effective only when everyone learns to pull together. You must understand team dynamics in order to ensure the success of your team.

ANALYZING TEAM DYNAMICS

Good team leaders make the most of the human assets at their disposal. To do this, you need to understand each group member, how their behaviour changes within the team, and how individual responses vary at different stages in the team's development.

39 Help your team find a way to change obstructive group behaviour.

POINTS TO REMEMBER

- Teams should spend as much time together as possible within working hours.
- People need to be comfortable to work well together.
- Negative behaviour within a team needs to be wiped out at the earliest opportunity.
- Insecurity is the enemy of team excellence and good management.
- The underlying causes of trouble should be dealt with at once.

ENCOURAGING TEAMWORK

Humans operate well in groups – a characteristic that can be seen in sporting teams, in which people instinctively co-operate, voluntarily take on responsibility, and endorse decisions for the overall good of the team. To achieve the same cohesive behaviour in a work environment, team members need to overcome any inclination to be defensive with each other. Encourage your team to spend as much time together as possible – humans are naturally gregarious creatures and will overcome any initial reticence as they grow to recognize each other's particular skills and strengths.

UNDERSTANDING TEAM DEVELOPMENT

A team grows and changes markedly during its lifetime. The process of development has been described as having four stages: forming, storming, norming, and performing. All teams pass through the initial stage of being brought together as a group. This is a tentative period that can easily develop into a "storming" phase in which people are unsure of each other and confused, and may become aggressive at times. With strong leadership, methods of working can be fully agreed in the "norming" stage, before the team goes on to perform at its best for the duration of its project.

40 Look for ways to use conflict constructively.

41 Remember that everyone deserves some fun during work hours.

DEALING WITH STAGES IN THE LIFE OF A TEAM

FORMING
Members are uncertain about roles, rules, and expectations

Use socializing and team discussion to initiate group work

STORMING
Members come into conflict over goals and personalities

Assert your authority to defuse conflict in the team

Encourage team members to establish a creative work pattern

NORMING
Working styles are agreed and systems set up

Build up team faith in their collective ability and skills

PERFORMING
Team works positively, creatively, and productively together

Allow individuals and sub-groups to act on their own initiative

USING MANAGING TACTICS

There are various management styles, but often successful management – and improving team efficiency – hinges on your ability to adapt your style to the changing needs and dynamics within a team as it develops. Team management tactics may vary from the autocratic to the liberal, but even the most tolerant and sharing of leaders needs to be able to control their team. Firm leadership is the foundation of collaborative, co-operative, and efficient teamwork.

42 Always conduct a thorough, open analysis when projects go wrong.

43 Have an open-door policy if you want to be accessible.

44 Ask people who bring you problems to bring solutions.

FORMING A TEAM

The formative stage of any project is always slightly experimental, and a team can be an excellent testing ground for new ideas. Although experiments should be worked out with care to give them a fair chance of success, a major part of teamwork is knowing how to recognize mistakes early and then to move to correct defects without anger or recrimination. Dealing with failed experiments is part of the learning process summed up in the "forming to performing" progression. Remember that different solutions are required at varying stages of the team's development.

◄ USING THE BEST PEOPLE

It is important to remember that the individuals initiating a project may not be the ones to see it through to the end. Here, different skills were introduced into the team at different stages, as one individual could not perform as implementer, sales person, and producer. The result was success for the whole team.

CASE STUDY

Jenny headed up the new venture team within her company and came up with an idea for a line of stationery. She passed her idea to the marketing department, who seemed to get nowhere with selling the product internally. Jenny went to a colleague, Peter, who was known to be a good decision-maker, and got him to further her cause.

Peter joined up with Anna, a good implementer of ideas, and they formed a new venture team. Together they personally took the new stationery line around to all their senior managers, selling the idea and convincing the managers to put capital into the project. Before they went into production of the stationery, they realized that they needed a line manager whose management style they liked and who could keep costs down. They recruited James to the team temporarily to set up the manufacturing process.

RESOLVING CONFLICT

In the "storming" part of the life of a team, conflicts can take place between:

● The leader and individual team members;
● The leader and the whole team;
● Individual team members.

These conflicts can be emotional, factual, constructive, destructive, argumentative, open, or suppressed. Try to resolve any disputes among team members by replacing emotive approaches to a problem with rational, open-minded ones.

45 Meet informally as well as formally to discuss your team's progress.

46 Use dispassionate fact-finding as the best method of defusing conflict.

ADAPTING YOUR ROLE

During the development of a team, changes in the management role occur. In the first instance, the team leader is predominantly an organizer who puts the team together. As the team settles, your role changes to that of counsellor or trouble-shooter. When the team is functioning – or "norming" – inspirational leadership is required to maintain momentum. During the final phase, "performing", act as facilitator to keep the team's wheels turning.

DEVELOPING MEMBERS' ROLES

It is not only the nature of teams that change over time – so do the abilities of the members as they build on their personal skills. With experience, indivduals learn how to be team members, solve problems, and work together successfully. At each stage of the development of your team, set challenging goals, review its working methods, and question its achievements to improve overall performance.

DO'S AND DON'TS

✔ Do change your leadership style according to the needs of your team.

✔ Do stress and support the values established by your team.

✔ Do be seen to react positively to novel and creative ideas.

✔ Do encourage individual and group learning at every stage of the team's development.

✘ Don't always dismiss conflict as somebody else's fault – look to see if you are to blame.

✘ Don't shirk any issues in which you feel strong management is needed for success.

✘ Don't let "not invented here" kill promising new initiatives.

✘ Don't miss the times when your leadership qualities are needed by your team.

COMMUNICATING EFFECTIVELY

Strong communication links are vital to the wellbeing of a team. The most effective links occur naturally – for example, in casual conversation – but these will need supplementing by new technology. Choose the most appropriate method to suit your team.

47 Keep the team members in close proximity to ease communication.

48 Set aside areas in which people can meet and talk informally.

ENSURING ACCESSIBILITY

How a team communicates internally depends on its size and the location of its members. The most effective method of communication is informal direct conversation and for this, ideally, team members should have easy access to each other at all times – preferably sitting close together. If certain members of a team are situated off-campus, establish efficient communication links, such as telephone, fax, e-mail, or video, between all the locations to ensure that dialogue can still flow freely between the parties concerned.

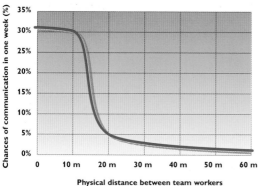

◀ ENCOURAGING COMMUNICATION
Physical distance has a great effect on levels of communication between team members. Research shows that if team members are seated less than 10 m (33 ft) apart, they have a 30 per cent chance of communicating at least once a week. This probability dwindles to a mere 5 per cent when people are seated more than 20 m (66 ft) apart and falls to virtually nothing when seated at a distance of 60 m (195 ft) or more apart.

COMMUNICATION METHODS

There are many ways for a team to communicate, whether formally or informally, within its own organization or externally. These include:

● Constant casual conversational links between colleagues. These create an informal "grapevine" throughout the organization;

● Traditional methods of communication such as paper memos, circulars, letters, reports, noticeboards, faxes, and telephone calls;

● Electronic means, such as e-mail, intranet (in-company e-mails), Internet, and groupware facilities (software packages tailored to groups);

● Video-conferencing facilities and video telephones that can reach right across the international business world.

Whichever communication systems are used, remember that they are all a supplement to, rather than a substitute for, face-to-face meetings.

49 Encourage the free flow of communication between colleagues.

50 Invest in the most appropriate technology, and keep it up to date.

POINTS TO REMEMBER

● E-mail can be used as an informal medium between team members, but confidentiality is not assured.

● Software packages can be tailored by specialist consultants to match the communication needs of any team.

● Video-conferences are useful communication tools that allow participants to assess each other's body language and mood.

● Video links are a cost-effective alternative to sending team members overseas for meetings.

● A good telephone system will have facilities for conference calls for use among members of teams sited in different locations.

CHOOSING METHODS OF COMMUNICATION

In any organization, many modes of communication exist side-by-side. You cannot stop the "grapevine" from working – indeed, it is one of the faster and thus more efficient methods of communication – so use it to your advantage by talking informally to all colleagues. If you want to reach your team or your whole organization quickly, use electronic means, such as e-mail. Video communications emulate the collaborative, informal style of true teamwork closely, as you can see the reactions of the people you are dealing with, so try these when your team is spread across a distance. Remember that traditional communications, such as memos and noticeboards, still have their place. For example, anybody can use noticeboards to share information that has not reached them personally.

RUNNING TEAM MEETINGS

Making team meetings effective is a major test of leadership skills. The key to holding a productive meeting is to involve everybody actively in the proceedings. Ensure that team members understand the purpose of each meeting and what is expected of them.

51 Change the chairperson at each meeting to involve everybody.

FULFILLING YOUR PURPOSE

Meetings should always have a clear purpose over and beyond the exchange of information. Determine the purpose of each meeting carefully – for example, is it to plan future action, or discuss a new recruit? Draw up an agenda listing the points to be discussed and distribute this in advance of the meeting so that people know why they are attending and can gather their thoughts beforehand. Lead the discussion and make your purpose clear, but aim to achieve consensus within the team.

▲ **KNOWING YOUR AIMS**
Be clear about what you need to achieve in a meeting: draw up an agenda and follow it closely. Go armed with all relevant facts and figures, and encourage team members to do the same.

52 Try to delegate as much as possible to other members of the team.

CONSIDERING FREQUENCY

Team and progress meetings should be held at least once every two weeks, so that the group's plans and deadlines stay clear in everyone's mind and the lines of communication remain open. Other types of meeting, such as confidential one-to-ones, focus groups, work-outs, and reporting meetings that are aimed at solving or discussing specific problems should be held as and when required.

PACING MEETINGS

When running a meeting, pace yourself with the aid of a pre-prepared agenda. Group similar topics together on the agenda to avoid repetition, allocate a time limit to each point to be discussed, and adhere to it strictly. Ask for ideas to be prepared in advance to save time in the meeting. Start proceedings promptly, and keep them moving – 75 minutes is enough to cover most agendas, and people lose concentration beyond that length of time. Encourage everybody to have their say, subject to relevance and reasonable brevity, as the livelier a meeting, the more creative the ideas generated.

53 Distribute agendas in advance of the meeting to give your team time to prepare.

MATCHING PURPOSE TO MEETING TYPE

MEETING TYPE	CHARACTERISTICS
TEAM MEETING Regular update meeting for whole team.	• Indispensable for teamwork: allows everyone a chance to find out how other team members are progressing. • Run freely by team leader to allow fruitful discussion.
FOCUS GROUP Meeting of sub-group with specific knowledge.	• Ideal for problem-solving, as all the people involved know the issues at stake and discuss them from an informed point of view. • As everyone is well-informed, does not require a leader.
PROGRESS MEETING Regular update meeting for sub-group of team.	• To set agenda at start of day or week. • Used to review and alter agenda for a set period of time. • Run tightly by team leader to maximize time usage.
ONE-TO-ONE Private meeting held between two people.	• Can be informal or formal. • May cover any topic, work-related or personal, including confidential matters, which may not be recorded.
WORK-OUT MEETING Meeting of whole group to study work methods.	• For examining and improving work methods and processes. • Involves a free discussion across the whole team. • Generates practical, quick solutions to problems encountered.
REPORTING MEETING Meeting to spread specific information to team.	• Allows the spread of information among team members. • Meeting is run by the presenter of the information. • Team leader acts as chief inquisitor to verify the information.

NETWORKING A TEAM

All teams, no matter what their purpose, depend to a considerable extent on good networking skills. Make full use of the formal and informal connections both inside and outside your organization to provide valuable support for your team.

54 Cultivate all relationships that may be useful to the team.

55 Try to keep all team relationships on an even keel.

UNDERSTANDING THE NEED FOR SUPPORT

All teams need friends in high places – a network system. At the top end of an organization, a network may include a decision-maker, such as a top executive; an influencer, who may have the ear of senior managers; one or more players, whose own tasks depend on your team's performance; and a consent-giver – an individual whose consent is officially required for key purposes. Remember to network in and outside the organization to find the support your team needs to function efficiently.

UNDERSTANDING ▼ OUTSIDE INFLUENCES
Specific individuals can exert considerable influence on your team from outside. Be aware of their impact upon the team, and seek their support and approval.

DECISION-MAKER
Has the power of veto over the team

INFLUENCER
May have influence on senior managers

PLAYER
Aids team by giving functional help

CONSENT-GIVER
Provides needed approval to the team

Team relies on influence and support from experts outside and inside the organization

FINDING SPONSORS

A team sponsor is usually a well-placed, well-disposed individual, working from either inside or outside an organization, who does not occupy any of the main four roles (decision-maker, influencer, player, or consent-giver) that affect a team. When a start-up runs into difficulties, or a crisis develops later in a team's life, turn to your sponsor for their ability to use influence on the four role-fillers. The sponsor's function is to help resolve an impasse or head off conflict. Team life is much tougher without such mentors.

56 Make sure that good news is heard and clearly understood by all the relevant people.

REMOVING WORK-RELATED PROBLEMS

57 If trouble is brewing in any team relationship, deal with it quickly.

Barriers to the success of team performance can be caused by the inflexibility of corporate tradition. Be aware of any company rules, regulations, and procedures that can cause delays and difficulties for the team. Look to your sponsor and network of contacts in senior management to smooth the passage of team decisions and actions through the organization. Such allies may be able to influence reticent colleagues and speed up approval processes.

DEALING WITH PROBLEM INDIVIDUALS

Watch out for the human factor: problems within the team can equally well be caused by outsiders. Work pressures, conservatism, jealousy, self-protection, or stubbornness can all drive individuals outside a team to try to disrupt its efficiency. Although many such situations can be resolved informally, avoid head-on conflict if you can. Ask an influencer, decision-maker, or team sponsor to deal with extreme cases personally. If trouble-makers persist in causing problems, look to senior management to resolve the situation.

POINTS TO REMEMBER

● The higher-placed a team's allies, the better the chance of success for the team.

● Time should be allocated to maintaining a network of influencers and sponsors.

● Sponsors need to be informed of team progress and consulted regularly for their advice.

● Anyone with influence over a senior decision-maker should be regarded with respect and caution.

SHARING INFORMATION OUTSIDE A TEAM

No person and no team is an island. Two-way information links between a team, the rest of an organization, and its external support are vital for efficiency. Remember that collaboration and co-operation are hindered by the absence of open communication.

58 Arrange social contacts with other parts of the organization.

COMMUNICATING FROM INSIDE

The natural tendency of teams is for their innate strength – their togetherness – to become a weakness: they may become clannish, keeping themselves and their information to themselves. Where work can be carried out in isolation, this may not matter, but most teams depend to some extent on other departments and functions within an organization, for example, for back-up, such as computer support, or when needing specialist help in, say, production or engineering.

59 Find out which technology can keep you in touch with sponsors.

POINTS TO CONSIDER BEFORE SPREADING INFORMATION

Is the information accurate?	*Double-check all available facts and figures*
Who needs to know this information?	*Always inform more people rather than less*
How is it best communicated?	*Consider complexity of material to be communicated*
Who communicates the information?	*Choose a qualified, experienced person to spread message*
Should any action follow?	*Know the purpose of spreading information*
Do you need to follow up afterwards?	*Set a deadline for follow-up to information*

MAINTAINING CONTACT

Keep a list of key people in other departments and outside the organization, making sure that everybody who needs to know particular information is included. Update and refine this list constantly, as different people and skills will be required to support a team at differing stages of its life. Use memos, faxes, letters, e-mail, video links, or "groupware" – software that ranges from electronic mail to complete networking systems – to enable members of the team to stay in touch with each other and with the support system.

60 Keep a record of contacts with valuable people you meet outside the team or office.

61 Award team roles carefully so they do not overlap.

CONFIDENTIALITY

A truly efficient team should have no professional secrets between its members, and should keep confidential only those matters that members agree are in the best interests of the project. Before deciding what is confidential, ask "Who else needs to know this?", and "Would openness be damaging?". If the answers are *everybody* and *no*, then feel free to circulate the information. However, if there is a real need for secrecy, ensure that it is maintained absolutely.

AVOIDING DUPLICATION

Duplication of roles is a critical problem in large organizations. For example, two projects, each instigated by different departments for different reasons, may well overlap. To prevent this waste of resources, circulate a brief covering your team's function to all relevant people. The overlap will soon be discovered if information is circulating properly. In some cases, it may be possible for the separate projects to benefit by uniting their efforts, or it may be constructive to combine results when both teams have completed their work.

CASCADING INFORMATION

One popular method of passing information down the line is the cascade, in which a chief executive briefs an executive committee, who briefs divisional heads, and so on. The more layers there are, the greater the danger that the cascading message can be distorted. Even without any factual distortion, comprehension and perception may differ from the original intention, and this can confuse a team's aims and its efficiency. To prevent this, hold large meetings rather than many small ones, and then, if necessary, feed an agreed summary back upwards.

THINKING CREATIVELY

Without new ideas, teams are unlikely to achieve the breakthroughs that generate real success. Creative thinking is a team responsibility in which all members should participate. Develop it in teams through plenty of training and practice.

62 Look for the good points in an idea, and never criticize ideas in public.

63 Look for people with experience when seeking problem-solvers.

64 Analyze the roles that people play within your team.

ENCOURAGING CREATIVITY

Many people become locked into patterns of thinking drawn from their own experience and personalities. To unlock their creativity, do not allow yourself or your team members to become typecast as creative or non-creative. Everybody is capable of having or developing new ideas. Encourage people to think creatively by insisting that they come to appropriate meetings – to discuss new products, for example, or to solve a problem – with a number of ideas. Then all can play a creative role, which emphasizes that thinking is a team activity in which everybody shares. Always welcome diversity of views and ideas, but steer debate towards consensus.

CASE STUDY

Harry is a clothing manufacturer. One of his best customers had placed a large order that seemed to be impossible to meet without diverting workers from jobs for other clients. He called together the whole executive team to look for a solution to the problem. Carlo, the head of manufacturing, wanted to hire tailors on a temporary basis to fill the order. The finance director, Jane, regarded this as costly and uncertain, and suggested subcontracting the work to another supplier. Ellen, from marketing, asked if anybody had contacted the customers to see if deliveries could be re-scheduled. Carlo immediately saw that, given this leeway, he could organize production, and meet all the demands with little delay. All the customers agreed to the new schedules, the improved work flow actually cut costs, and everybody was satisfied.

◀ **TRYING A NEW PERSPECTIVE**
In this case, a company was in danger of losing money and face by not being able to complete an order. Drawing together people with different skills and ideas brought fresh solutions to the problem.

Ideas are brought to meeting

Team member contributes

All ideas are recorded on a flip chart

Leader

▲ WORKING TOGETHER

To achieve the most from a brainstorming session, make sure that the atmosphere between team members is amicable – more creative ideas will be produced if attendees are relaxed and have no qualms about speaking in front of each other.

POINTS TO REMEMBER

- Brainstorming is sometimes called "group action thinking".
- Criticism kills creativity. Ideas should never be scorned during a brainstorming session.
- Many seemingly foolish ideas can lead to sensible solutions.
- All ideas should be recorded – no matter how unconventional they appear to be.
- The joint creative input in these sessions will always be higher than individuals can provide alone.

GENERATING NEW IDEAS

Brainstorming sessions aim to generate as many ideas as possible, no matter how far-fetched. They can be used for many purposes, from new ways to market a product, to devising a new pay system. Brainstorming requires a leader and takes some organization – a session should be open-ended, but the leader should call a halt when it starts to run out of steam. All ideas should be recorded on a flip chart or white board so they can be seen by everyone. Afterwards, reject non-starters and produce a shortlist of feasible ideas. Use this as the agenda for a subsequent meeting to discuss and agree on the best idea and action plan.

65 Never dismiss brainstormed ideas out of hand – that is disheartening and stops the flow of creativity.

DEALING WITH PROBLEMS

Team members not only solve problems – they also create them. It is vital to build up loyalty between team members so that all difficulties, whether personal, work-related, or procedural, are tackled before they undermine the collective team spirit.

66 Treat everyone in the team equally to avoid causing any resentment.

INSTILLING TEAM SPIRIT

That indefinable quality known as team spirit can be encouraged in a number of ways:

● Let team members know why they were chosen for their particular task;
● Establish a common team purpose and specific goals to challenge the strengths of the team;
● Encourage the team to communicate well, and always praise wherever praise is due;
● Ask your team for its advice, and then be seen to act upon it;
● Take the time to respond in detail to reports and information coming from your team.

◀ PROVIDING FEEDBACK
Team spirit is encouraged by a feeling of mutual trust and open communication. Always be ready to give praise to team members, and listen carefully to what they have to say to you.

IDENTIFYING PROBLEMS

All teams have a latent difficulty. You want the individuals to act as a unit, but they may disagree with each other or with the direction of the team. Ask questions to establish whether problems are localized (one or two people) or a sign of general dissatisfaction. If the morale of the whole team is unsatisfactory and therefore damaging its work, there is no alternative but to rethink your strategy, how the team is structured, and who is in it.

67 Regard disruptive team members as innocent until they are proven guilty.

TALKING TO INDIVIDUALS

Once a problem is identified, it is an inevitable and important part of team leadership to discuss it with the people involved. This is pre-eminently a listening task – let them tell you how they see what is happening. At the same time, use your prior knowledge of them, and any observations made during meetings, to assess their attitudes and preconceptions. What they say and what they do and feel may be different things. Do they have hidden agendas? Are they withholding any information and/or emotions that run deep? Their reactions will tell you whether their commitment to the group and its objectives is strong. If it is, they will genuinely want to find the root of the problem as much as you do, and will be happy to co-operate with you fully. If an individual blames others and plunges into self-justification, confront and question this defensive reaction.

POINTS TO REMEMBER

- Personal problems between members of a team should be handled in a constructive way.
- It is not sensible to react to any difficulties until you are sure that you know the real cause.
- There are always new mountains for any team to climb.
- A "blame culture" must be prevented from developing – otherwise, it will kill team spirit.

68 Telling individuals they are doing a good job will build team morale.

LEADING TEAMS FROM THE FRONT

Your team looks to you to provide cohesion and inspiration. Be aware of this, and lead them from the front by:

- Raising team sights continually: the higher the realistic aims, the greater the shared excitement of the team hitting the target – which will instil a sense of urgency and drive in the members;
- Recognizing and celebrating group or individual successes as they occur;
- Using your own interpersonal skills to pull the team together. Be confident and highly visible. Develop an accessible style to which people can relate – this will promote ease of communication.

▲ ENCOURAGING PEOPLE

To instil and maintain confidence in team members, always make obvious your enthusiasm for the project in hand and your faith in the team.

DEALING WITH PROBLEM PEOPLE

After you speak to people causing a problem within a team, further action may be needed. Be positive, and search for any common ground from which to start rebuilding relations. Are roles within the team unclear, causing overlap of responsibility? Is the workload fairly distributed, or are certain individuals feeling overburdened and stressed? In both cases, rethink the allocation of the workload. Experiment to find solutions to the problems, but remember to act in good time. You must remove people from a team if you find that their disruptive behaviour persists after all avenues have been explored.

69 Always treat team members with respect, even those who may be creating problems for you.

DO'S & DON'TS

✔ Do tell the truth about how you see a situation.	✘ Don't persist with impossible people.
✔ Do try to see a problem from your team's angle.	✘ Don't lose your own temper with any members of the team.
✔ Do use the problem as a lever for change.	✘ Don't lose sight of the team's purpose.
✔ Do be positive when handling problems.	✘ Don't hesitate to call on outside help where you feel it is necessary.
✔ Do tackle problems head on, rather than delaying your action.	✘ Don't cause more problems by ignoring tensions in your team.

70 Avoid direct conflict with team members.

71 Remember to be tough on the problems, not the people.

DEALING WITH CONFLICT

Head-on personal conflict between team members soon becomes a problem for the entire team. Address such situations as soon as they arise. Offer one or two team members the opportunity to tell you, in confidence, what they perceive as the root of the clash, and explore ways of defusing the situation. How many people are causing the conflict? Is one individual behaving badly? Talk to them personally. Has the team become divided? If so, insist on a truce between the warring parties. Is your management at fault? If so, talk to team members to see how you can redress the situation. The object of the exercise is to improve behaviour, not parcel out blame and criticism. Do not rest until a solution has been found and agreed by all.

USING A PROBLEM LOG

Regard work-related problems as opportunities for team learning and improvement. Enter the issue in a log, and allow all team members access to the log so that the lessons learned can be shared. Select an individual to resolve the problem, and give them the necessary authority and resources. Ask for a plan of action and regular progress reports. Record these reports in the log, noting any problems and the final resolution.

72 Ensure that the whole team is able to learn from solving problems.

LEARNING FROM PROBLEM-SOLVING

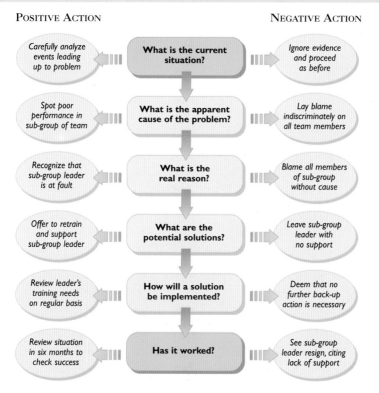

POSITIVE ACTION		NEGATIVE ACTION
Carefully analyze events leading up to problem	**What is the current situation?**	Ignore evidence and proceed as before
Spot poor performance in sub-group of team	**What is the apparent cause of the problem?**	Lay blame indiscriminately on all team members
Recognize that sub-group leader is at fault	**What is the real reason?**	Blame all members of sub-group without cause
Offer to retrain and support sub-group leader	**What are the potential solutions?**	Leave sub-group leader with no support
Review leader's training needs on regular basis	**How will a solution be implemented?**	Deem that no further back-up action is necessary
Review situation in six months to check success	**Has it worked?**	See sub-group leader resign, citing lack of support

IMPROVING STANDARDS IN A TEAM

*A*ny systematic approach to improving *performance needs to challenge existing ways of working. Teams looking to improve must learn to generate their own tasks, tackle problems, agree on solutions, and implement their decisions with confidence.*

73 Go for some large, quick, quality wins to encourage further effort.

KNOWING THE PROJECT

People in true teams "own" their jobs – they are each responsible for finding the best methods of performing excellent work to the highest possible standard. A manufacturing cell goes one step beyond this: team members are multi-skilled and know each team role well enough to take it over. Such flexibility can strengthen any team. Teams gain greatly by studying the progress of other people's jobs. Track your team's project "end-to-end" to gain a better understanding of the task, your role, other team roles, how to improve performance, and how such improvement will pay off.

▼ **KEEPING TRACK OF PERFORMANCE**

Track the progress of a team project from beginning to end to see what pitfalls and problems are encountered. Talk to individual team members to understand the problems they have faced and make a note of how these were solved.

Leader asks team member pertinent questions and notes answers

Team member describes problem and solution

IMPROVING SYSTEMS

The Japanese management technique of *kaizen* holds that everybody and every team can improve the quality of their work continually by valuable and quantifiable amounts. Even a small fall in the percentage of rejected products, for example, can mean big savings in production costs. Give teams complete responsibility for their task, so that they can set the improvement process underway by defining problems, analyzing the root cause, improving the situation – perhaps by bringing in external specialist help, if necessary – and, above all, preventing the problem from recurring.

74 Ensure that team members know about other roles within the group.

75 Work out the cost of failure before the cost of quality.

76 Build significant improvement targets into every budget and every team action plan.

MAINTAINING A FRESH APPROACH

As teams develop and settle into a routine, they often fall into set patterns of behaviour and group thinking. Avoid the temptation to leave a situation well alone on the grounds that change serves little purpose: strive for continual improvement to challenge the viability of a team's assumptions and working practices. How can you improve team performance? Have you overlooked anything that can be improved? Do you need new blood in the team? Is the product still right for the market?

CHALLENGING COMMON ASSUMPTIONS

Challenge any perceived assumptions in order to improve team practice:
● "Tackling the symptom cures the disease". Remember that problems will recur if not tackled at root level;
● "Problems and their solutions are always isolated". Bear in mind that secondary, knock-on effects can be

worse than the primary consequences;
● "Quality comes expensive". Remember that improving quality makes economic sense when measured against the direct and indirect costs of failure;
● "Quality applies only to products". Apply quality to every service and process in which your team is involved.

RATING TEAM LEADERSHIP

Team leadership is a many-sided process, as the following self-assessment shows. If you are currently leading a team, this will test the quality of your working methods and ability to manage people. If you are a team member, test your own leadership potential. Be as honest as you can: if your answer is "never", mark Option 1; if it is "always", mark Option 4; and so on. Add your scores together, and refer to the Analysis to see how you scored. Use your answers to identify the areas that need improving.

OPTIONS
1 Never
2 Occasionally
3 Frequently
4 Always

1 I share the leadership role with other members of the team.

1   2   3   4

2 I encourage team members to set themselves genuinely stretching tasks.

1   2   3   4

3 I meet with internal and external customers to ensure that they are satisfied.

1   2   3   4

4 I socialize with the team to build team spirit and exchange views informally.

1   2   3   4

5 I give credit when credit is due and do not hesitate to criticize if necessary.

1   2   3   4

6 I have an inner team of deputies and consult with them on team progress.

1   2   3   4

7 I give the team and its members precise goals and communicate them clearly.

1   2   3   4

8 I keep in touch with team sponsors to keep external relations smooth.

1   2   3   4

9 I try to show the members of my team that I trust them implicitly.

1   2   3   4

10 I explain why if I have to reject a team member's idea on solving a problem.

1   2   3   4

11 I turn whole tasks over to the team to carry out as the members see fit.

1   2   3   4

12 I allow my team to have a say in any decision that affects it.

1   2   3   4

13 I ask individuals on the team what they think about current working methods.

1   2   3   4

14 I look for the underlying causes of any problems that arise within my team.

1   2   3   4

15 I deliberately change my management style to suit changing situations.

1   2   3   4

16 I encourage team members to come to me with any problems.

1   2   3   4

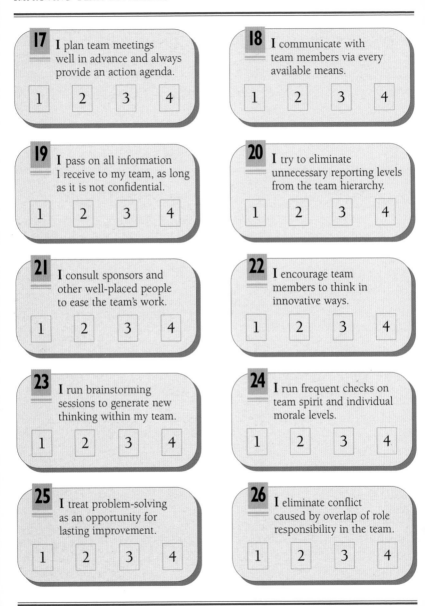

17 I plan team meetings well in advance and always provide an action agenda.

1   2   3   4

18 I communicate with team members via every available means.

1   2   3   4

19 I pass on all information I receive to my team, as long as it is not confidential.

1   2   3   4

20 I try to eliminate unnecessary reporting levels from the team hierarchy.

1   2   3   4

21 I consult sponsors and other well-placed people to ease the team's work.

1   2   3   4

22 I encourage team members to think in innovative ways.

1   2   3   4

23 I run brainstorming sessions to generate new thinking within my team.

1   2   3   4

24 I run frequent checks on team spirit and individual morale levels.

1   2   3   4

25 I treat problem-solving as an opportunity for lasting improvement.

1   2   3   4

26 I eliminate conflict caused by overlap of role responsibility in the team.

1   2   3   4

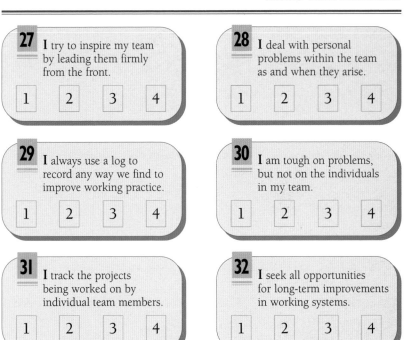

27 I try to inspire my team by leading them firmly from the front.

1 2 3 4

28 I deal with personal problems within the team as and when they arise.

1 2 3 4

29 I always use a log to record any way we find to improve working practice.

1 2 3 4

30 I am tough on problems, but not on the individuals in my team.

1 2 3 4

31 I track the projects being worked on by individual team members.

1 2 3 4

32 I seek all opportunities for long-term improvements in working systems.

1 2 3 4

ANALYSIS

Now you have completed the assessment, add up your total score, and check your performance by reading the corresponding evaluation below. Whatever level of success you have achieved, or have the potential to achieve, there is always room for improvement. Identify your weakest areas, and refer to the relevant sections of this book, where you will find practical advice and tips that will enable you to establish and hone team leadership skills.

32–63: You are not keeping up with the pace of change. Look for ways to update your management style.

64–95: Some of your leadership qualities are good, so concentrate on improving weak areas.

96–128: This is the zone of excellence, but do not let that lull you into complacency – strive to improve.

WORKING FOR THE FUTURE

Identifying new challenges for an established team is one of the most exciting aspects of teamwork. Use appropriate techniques to drive the team forwards to bigger and better targets.

MEASURING PERFORMANCE

If something cannot be measured, it cannot be improved upon. This basic principle applies to any job. Define individual and team standards – that they always meet deadlines, for instance – to give a targeted objective by which performance can be judged.

77 Tell each member of a team which measurements set the standards.

78 Ensure that all improvements and new targets are maintained.

CHOOSING MEASURES

Every team effort contains some elements that can be measured by performance. Look for wide-ranging measures when analyzing performance. Measure those standards whose improvement will ensure real economic benefits. For instance, if a call-centre team is measured only by the number of calls handled per hour, the quality of response may suffer. Setting a quota of calls per hour and a waiting-time target, monitoring a percentage of calls, and surveying customer satisfaction by making follow-up calls will be a more effective way of raising team performance.

ASSESSING RESULTS

Teamwork can benefit from having performance measured by the team members themselves. They can generally be trusted to assess their own achievement levels accurately and understand the implications. Make sure that the data used is "robust" – that is, any measures you are assessing are meaningful and accurate. Input data on to appropriate computer software to save time and interpret the results effectively. Also, use independent outside assessors if you need specific facts, such as comparative market shares of products in competition with your own.

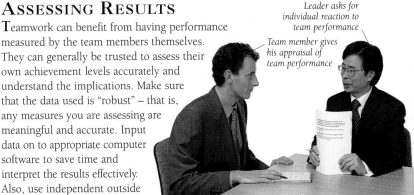

Leader asks for individual reaction to team performance

Team member gives his appraisal of team performance

▲ DISCUSSING TEAM RESULTS

When measuring the performance of a team, ask each member for their opinion of how targets were handled, if working methods could be improved, and whether the results are realistic.

MEASURING STAFF PERFORMANCE

WHO TO MEASURE	ASPECTS TO MEASURE
WHOLE TEAM Measure the progress of the whole team against the project objectives, schedules, and budgets.	● Finance: actual expenditure; profit versus forecasts. ● Time: physical output and tasks achieved versus schedule. ● Quality: accuracy; customer satisfaction. ● Development: investment in teamwork; technical skills.
LEADER Measure the effectiveness of the team leader in providing support and direction to the team.	● Control: achievement of results as planned or budgeted. ● Upward appraisal: performance as rated by team. ● Downward appraisal: performance as rated by superiors. ● Morale: ratings by team members, customers, or suppliers.
SUB-GROUP Evaluate the effectiveness of each sub-group within the main team in meeting the set objectives.	● Targets: actual results versus objectives. ● Quality: level as assessed by internal customers. ● Customer: performance as assessed by external customers. ● Improvement: plans for better results in future.
TEAM MEMBERS Assess the contribution of each individual to the achievement of the objectives of the team.	● Output: performance against targets. ● Appraisal: rating by superiors, colleagues, and customers. ● Self-appraisal: own rating as individual and team member. ● Added value: contribution outside specific, defined duties.

TRACKING TEAM PROGRESS

A good team is aware of the need to remain dynamic. Review progress regularly to maintain momentum, provide an overview, and ask team members, singly or in groups, to define specific aspects of the project that could be improved in the future.

79 Circulate all relevant facts and figures before team reviews.

80 Never make personal attacks on individuals during reviews.

HOLDING TEAM REVIEWS

Regular team reviews strengthen teamwork and provide impetus for further progress. They can be conducted by the entire team or by key team members. Use them to check team performance against team objectives and any valid comparisons – such as the results of competitors. Check work methods to see if they are still appropriate, and consider what the next stages of action need to be. If necessary, delegate the development of any necessary action plans to experienced people.

Team communicates well at outset of project

Team performance declines due to poor communication

REVIEWING PROGRESS ▲

This illustration shows two possible outcomes of the career of a team – negative and positive. Despite starting out well, it is easy for a team to let personal problems hinder their progress. To stay on course, maintain constant, open communication.

Team fails to achieve target

HIGHLIGHTING OBSTACLES

As a team becomes established, every team activity can be seen as a distinct process. Tracking these processes almost always reveals ways in which time and money can be saved and quality improved. This is a valuable teamwork exercise, both for results and for the discussion involved in achieving them. For example, a team may draw up a flowchart showing how customer orders result in final delivery. Each activity and all decision points are marked on the diagram. If the flowchart reveals a bottleneck, the team draws a diagram of causes and effects, then resolves or improves the situation.

81 Remember that relationships will change over time.

82 Avoid the trap of minimizing or ignoring bad news.

Team achieves targets

Team holds regular reviews

Individuals discuss ways of improving performance

ACTING ON INFORMATION

In addition to information from reviews and the team's own analysis, a team may receive information from outside, such as a falling share of a particular market. In other cases, a team itself seeks new information – for example, customer reaction to proposed changes in its services. Some of this data-gathering is analytical: which activities generate what costs, which products make money. To remain dynamic, the team needs to use this information to change and improve. Encourage team members to look at the information and discard some activities, reduce some costs, raise some prices – and obtain better overall results.

TRAINING A TEAM

Training helps to improve the technical skills of team members and develop the managerial and interpersonal relations within a team. Review and upgrade the skills of a team constantly to meet current and future challenges successfully.

83 At the end of every day, ask if the team has moved forwards.

84 Listen to the feedback given by trainees about training courses.

ASSESSING COSTS

Despite the expense involved in training, it is cheaper than the cost of persisting without it, which will be damaging to performance. Calculate the costs of training, including training staff, materials, room hire, course fees, subsistence, travel, and loss of work hours. Weigh up these costs against the expected financial gains and improvements evident in team performance following training.

TRAINING TEAM MEMBERS

When trying to optimize the various skills in a team, involve the whole team in planning its own development. The aim is to reinforce the strengths and eliminate the weaknesses of all the team members, and develop those skills necessary to seize future opportunities and see off any threats. Discuss these aims with the whole team, draw up a training plan, and work out with each individual what his or her own needs are now and what will benefit projects and the team as a whole in the future.

Team member builds on existing skills

Team leader demonstrates new techniques

▲ **WORKING WITH TEAM MEMBERS**
Ask team members to evaluate their own skills and weaknesses. Encourage them to tell you where they feel they need more skills training – for example, in using specialist software. If you have relevant experience, set aside time to train them yourself.

TRAINING LEADERS

As a team leader, you should be exemplifying the qualities necessary to manage a team successfully. Ensure that you receive the requisite training to develop prioritizing, progress-chasing, delegation, and motivating skills. Make these an integral part of your personal development plan, and ensure that team members – especially your deputies – also develop their own leadership skills. Listening carefully, criticizing constructively, being tolerant of error while correcting mistakes, and retaining objectivity are leadership qualities that members should use within a team and in future projects.

85 Find the best and best-equipped training facilities.

86 Use consultants to develop in-house training courses.

87 Use mealtimes on away days to plan informally.

▼ **OFF-SITE WORKING**
Meeting off-site enables team members to maximize their time together creatively, pool ideas, and concentrate on training without any of the usual distractions.

USING AWAY-DAYS

From time to time, it can be helpful to take a team to a venue away from the workplace for a training session. Make sure that team members understand that you are planning a determined strategic work session and intend to keep firmly to the agenda. Bring in outsiders to give constructive criticism and advice. Leave the venue with an agreed action programme, and make sure that individuals are accountable for each aspect of its implementation.

SETTING TARGETS

Targets are vital to the whole teamwork process. They ensure that a product is delivered to the satisfaction of the customer, schedules and budgets are adhered to, and that standards are met. They are also the yardstick on which rewards can be based.

88 Involve everybody in target-setting to foster teamwork and consensus.

USING TARGETS TO MOTIVATE A TEAM

89 Motivate teams by allowing them to decide how to meet targets.

Successes, training, and learning are all highly motivational, and the same should be true of the way in which you communicate your expectations to your team. Motivate your team to reach specific goals by describing the ultimate set of targets as challenges that can be met through their own combined skills and effort. You can also increase team motivation by allowing members to form their own targets. Give them the opportunity to debate their aims in detail and discuss between themselves how aims can be met and possibly exceeded. It is highly motivational to set targets and succeed in outstripping them.

CASE STUDY

Elaine was a vital backroom figure in setting up a new call centre for dealing with customer enquiries. She was offered the chance to take on more responsibility, and given the option of three projects in which to become involved. She chose to work in a team monitoring the number, type, and handling of queries that came in from the public.

Having realized that some callers were not receiving the information they wanted, Elaine gave herself six months in which to reach the target of 90 per cent customer satisfaction with response to the calls from the public. She began to reorganize the company's research facility and to speed up reaction times to the phone calls and improve the manner in which they were handled. She was highly motivated by the challenge she had set herself, and a marked improvement in customer satisfaction was soon obvious.

◀ **MOTIVATING INDIVIDUALS**
The challenge of being in a more responsible role, and the desire to see the project succeed, motivated an individual member of the team to set herself, and reach, an ambitious personal target.

STRETCHING TARGETS

The greatest challenge that you can present to a team is the "stretch" goal. This means setting a target that can be achieved only by using skills that extend the previous capabilities of the team. Even an already successful team can outperform its previous standards, as long as you provide them with appropriate back-up. Set a stretch target with concise, well thought-out, practical, financial, and economic aims. This will provide a whole set of subsidiary targets which you should then break down into individual goals and tasks.

90 Ensure that team targets enthuse team members, and change them if they do not.

91 A team without stretch goals will under-perform one that has them.

MODIFYING TARGETS

A target, stretch or not, involves a plan. If the plan is failing, and the targets are likely to be missed, find out why. Set up a meeting with the whole team to analyze the issue until you have pinpointed the problem. As a team, decide how to solve it, then do just that. Set new targets in line with the new situation. This may be more motivating than any previous plan, both because the team is solving the problem together and because, sometimes, the second-try plan improves on the original.

PHRASES TO USE TO MOTIVATE A TEAM

Remember that everybody responds best to constructive leadership. Never voice any doubt about the abilities of a team, and always show confidence in their ability to reach their targets, making each team member feel appreciated.

❝ I know that I'm asking for the impossible – but I also know that this team can do it. ❞

❝ Thanks for a terrific job – I think you are ready for something even bigger now. ❞

❝ Why did we fail to meet that target – do you think we need to revise our original plan? ❞

❝ If we can just get through this minor setback, reaching that target will seem like plain sailing. ❞

REWARDING PERFORMANCE

The object of a successful reward system is to motivate teams to improve their overall performance. Calculate rewards with care, and choose the most appropriate types. Financial and incentive-based schemes – or a combination of both – are popular.

92 Allow your staff to have a say when it comes to setting reward levels.

CULTURAL DIFFERENCES

National cultural differences on rewards and performance are narrowing as companies continue to spread globally. In the US, share ownership has become common in some industries, but it is still rare in Japan. Large Europe-wide groups are now tending towards rewarding staff with performance-linked pay.

BROADCASTING FIGURES

When targets and results are used to encourage and reward performance, both sets of relevant figures must be known and accepted by all the team. Publicize the numbers – whether by fax, memo, bulletin board, electronic means, or newsletter – and explain to everyone exactly how the reward system will work. Make sure that each team member understands the bonus system, has access to the targets they are expected to reach, and can see their actual performance figures. Only then will they appreciate what they are working towards and how they will benefit – both as a team and in an individual capacity.

SETTING REWARD LEVELS

It requires judgment and experience to set a reward system at just the right level. Fix too low a rate, and team effort and morale fall off. Be too generous, and you will not stretch the team. When calculating rewards, work out what you can reasonably expect from your team by looking at their past performance, and that of similar departments and organizations. As the team gains in experience and skill, you may need to raise your sights by setting a higher reward base in order to encourage team members to continue stretching themselves and performing at their best.

93 Avoid using league tables – the team member at the bottom will become resentful.

CHOOSING REWARDS

REWARD	IMPLEMENTATION	BENEFITS TO TEAM
PAY RISE Rise in salary not directly related to performance and with no direct teamwork element.	● Requires no extra action by the management above approval of overall salary scale and placing particular jobs within the scale. ● May go hand in hand with promotion up the job scale.	● Members of the team know where they stand financially. ● The uncertainty of variable payments is avoided. ● Can take away element of competition within team.
BONUS PAYMENT Can take several forms, including sharing of financial savings made as a result of team effort.	● Needs meaningful measures on which payments can be based. ● Can allow team to decide how gross sum should be divided. ● May reveal how members of the team regard each other.	● Members have incentive for cost-cutting and quality drives as the bonus paid out from team funds will increase. ● Acts as a good long-term motivator of individuals.
PROFIT-SHARING Usually a given share of the profits is split between employees, either on corporate or divisional basis.	● Management must find a fair method of profit distribution. ● If of equal benefit to whole team, need to confront the fact that individual performances are not being singled out.	● Profit-sharing is popular with employees and is a great motivator of individuals. ● Increases the sense of people belonging to a team working towards a common aim.
SHARE OWNERSHIP Rewarding team members with shares is moving down from senior levels in many corporations.	● Is directly linked to corporate results rather than individual staff performances. ● Helps to close the "us and them" gap between management and lower levels of staff.	● Pride of ownership encourages team spirit, but hinges on the share price, rather than team effort or success. ● Identifies team members with overall group results.
RECOGNITION REWARDS Possibilities are legion, ranging from formal prizes to holidays and parties.	● Management must be careful to avoid implying that doing a great job is the exception instead of the expectation. ● Encourages people to perform as rewards are motivational.	● Members love recognition, even if only verbal, and cost is often little or nothing. ● Can reward team or individual. ● The better these rewards, the better the team atmosphere.
COMPOSITE REWARDS Reward types are often combined for maximum team and individual effect.	● Should always include and emphasize individual recognition. ● Allows management to combine individual with company-wide rewards, with elements tied to teamwork.	● Reward packages stimulate and motivate: variation helps to keep interest fresh. ● All senior-level recognition of teamwork elements will help to boost team spirit and morale.

ADAPTING TO CHANGE

Managing change is fast becoming a dominant theme of management practice. The pace of change is accelerating as markets become more international and technological innovation increases. Ensure that teams adapt to external changes.

94 Appoint someone to monitor any relevant changes in the market.

ANTICIPATING CHANGE

95 Be prepared to change even the most fundamental elements of a plan.

Over the course of a team's life, it is inevitable that its tasks will change in terms of objectives, timescale, cost elements, or deadlines. To be successful, teams must be prepared to adapt quickly to new circumstances. External pressures may force changes within a team, and personnel may come and go. Make sure that team members recognize the need for change and are flexible enough to accept it, whatever form it may take.

ANALYZING TYPES OF CHANGE

TYPES OF CHANGE	EFFECTS OF CHANGE
STAFFING Team members leave and join; roles are reorganized.	● May involve a change in working practice, and a different set of objectives for the team as a whole. ● Provides an opportunity to demonstrate a fresh start.
MANAGEMENT New management strategies or policies affect team.	● Team may become responsible to a different department. ● External management supervision may intensify. ● Challenges team to prove its value by improved performance.
PROJECT Content of teamwork is radically altered.	● Internal or external circumstances force major change in the nature or timescale of project and undermine assumptions. ● Project may have to be restarted from scratch.
EFFICIENCY Leader takes a decision to improve team efficiency.	● Strengthens ability of team members to meet their targets. ● May require a new plan of action or restaffing. ● Emphasizes positive aspects of new approach.

KEEPING TEAMS INFORMED

If you announce changes with enthusiasm, teams will develop a more positive attitude towards the new. Tell people about change as soon as enough detail is known for most questions to be answered, and be open with your opinions, but – as with all communication – make it a two-way exercise. Change affects every member of a team, therefore everyone should be given the chance to react. Listen carefully to your team's reactions – the more involved the team is in any decisions, the more likely it is to accept change, however difficult.

▼ **MAKING PEOPLE AWARE OF CHANGE**
In order to avoid speculation and rumour about any upcoming changes, and to ensure that team members do not feel threatened, make a point of letting them know what is happening well in advance.

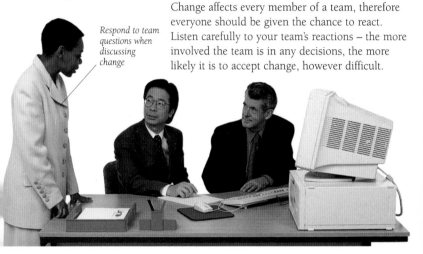

Respond to team questions when discussing change

SEIZING OPPORTUNITIES

Market fluctuations, technological advances, new competitors, or simply new tastes in the market may appear to pose a threat to teams, but even unwelcome changes can be used as a springboard for renewed progress. Try to analyze the proposed changes objectively. How can the drawbacks be offset or eliminated? How can the positive aspects be exploited? Follow this analysis by brainstorming alternative courses of action to deal with the change – and look for the plan that seems to offer the least disadvantage and the greatest opportunity for progress to everybody within the team.

96 Remember that some people are afraid of change.

97 Look for team members who can advance change.

PLANNING FUTURE GOALS FOR A TEAM

The vision that holds a team together does not end with the task in hand. Consider the future of the team both as a group and as individuals, as the career progress of each member is affected by their experience and success within the team.

| 98 | Conduct personal career progress appraisals at regular intervals. |

DEVELOPING YOUR TEAM

The main objective of any team is to work together to succeed at a given task, and this is facilitated if individual members are constantly increasing their own skills base. Good team leaders understand that the future success of a team depends entirely on how individuals develop. Act as both coach and career counsellor to the members of your team. Help to advance their careers by developing their natural talents and providing training and support, stretching challenges, and realistic targets. This will be of benefit to them and also to your team.

| 99 | Remember that encouragement of the individuals will help the team. |

LETTING PEOPLE GROW

The larger a team and the wider its remit, the greater the chance for individuals to develop their careers by changing roles or being promoted within the team. While promotion is usually vertical, team careers tend to progress horizontally: people move to larger teams or those handling higher-profile projects. Do not discourage this. Help promising colleagues to find suitable positions elsewhere, internally or externally. Even in organizations where vertical promotion is harder, individuals can still progress as they move from team to team.

| 100 | Agree career plans with team members and give them any support they need. |

Promoted to marketing director of the company

Headhunted as manager in company making that product

Made team leader due to specialized product knowledge

Promoted to manager of sales team with a budget of £10 million

Promoted to director of sales team with a budget of £100 million

Begins career selling new product in specific market

◀ **MAKING PROGRESS**

This chart shows two options for career progress. Following the traditional, vertical path, progress is made by moving from one organization to another and being promoted upwards. In the alternative, horizontal progress is made by moving to more powerful teams with bigger remits.

QUESTIONS TO ASK TEAM MEMBERS

Q Where do you want your career to be in ten years time?

Q Have you thought seriously about your career options?

Q Do you appreciate that, ultimately, the smooth progression of your career is in your own hands?

Q Have you considered the experience that you need to acquire to follow your chosen career path?

Q Are you aware that your contribution towards the success of your team will help advance your career?

BUILDING CAREERS

However helpful you and other senior colleagues are, individual team members must be aware that they have the overall responsibility for their own careers. Encourage each member to regard working on the team as part of a learning process, in which all lessons can open up new opportunities, thus building up a body of qualifications to take to their next position – whether in another team, a different department, or outside the organization. Career-building, like good teamwork, will always be more effective if it is targeted. Where do team members want to be by a certain age? What do they need to qualify for that position? Help them to act on the answers to these questions, and you are providing them with a stepping stone to success.

101 Keep in touch with team members after they disperse – you may well want to work with them again.

INDEX

ACKNOWLEDGMENTS

AUTHOR'S ACKNOWLEDGMENTS

This book owes its existence to the perceptive inspiration of Stephanie Jackson and Nigel Duffield at Dorling Kindersley; and I owe more than I can say to the expertise and enthusiasm of Jane Simmonds and all the editorial and design staff who worked on the project. I am also greatly indebted to the many colleagues, friends, and other management luminaries on whose wisdom and information I have drawn.

PUBLISHER'S ACKNOWLEDGMENTS

Dorling Kindersley would like to thank Jayne Jones and Emma Lawson for their valuable part in the planning and development of this series, everyone who generously lent props for the photoshoots, and the following for their help and participation:

Editorial Tracey Beresford, Deirdre Clark, Christopher Gordon, Adèle Hayward;
Design Ellen Woodward; **DTP assistance** Rachel Symons; **Consultant** Josephine Bryan;
Indexer Hilary Bird; **Proofreader** Helen Partington; **Photography** Steve Gorton;
Photographer's assistant Sarah Ashun; **Illustrators** Darren Hill, Jason Little;
Photographic co-ordinator Laura Watson.

Models Philip Argent, Marian Broderick, Angela Cameron, Kuo Kang Chen, Felicity Crowe,
Patrick Dobbs, Carole Evans, Vosjava Fahkro, John Gillard, Ben Glickman, Sasha Heseltine, Richard Hill,
Maggie Mant, Frankie Mayers, Sotiris Melioumis, Mutsumi Niwa, Kiran Shah, Lois Sharland, Lynne Staff,
Daniel Stevens, Gilbert Wu, Wendy Yun; **Make-up** Elizabeth Burrage.

Special thanks to the following for their help throughout the series:
Ron and Chris at Clark Davis & Co. Ltd for stationery and furniture supplies; Pam Bennett and
the staff at Jones Bootmakers, Covent Garden, for the loan of footwear; Alan Pfaff and the staff at
Moss Bros, Covent Garden, for the loan of the men's suits; David Bailey for his help and time;
Graham Preston and the staff at Staverton for their time and space.

Suppliers Austin Reed, Church & Co., Compaq, David Clulow Opticians,
Elonex, Escada, Filofax, Gateway 2000, Mucci Bags.

Picture researchers Victoria Peel, Sam Ruston; **Picture librarian** Sue Hadley.

PICTURE CREDITS

Key: *b* bottom, *c* centre, *l* left, *r* right, *t* top
Tony Stone Images: Bruce Ayres 4–5, 29*t*, 47*br*, Walter Hodges 8*b*, Michael Rosenfeld 61*b*.
Front cover **Tony Stone Images**: Bruce Ayres *cl*.

AUTHOR'S BIOGRAPHY

Robert Heller is a leading authority in the world of management consultancy and was the founding editor of Britain's top management magazine, *Management Today*. He is much in demand as a conference speaker in Europe, North and South America, and the Far East. As editorial director of Haymarket Publishing Group, Robert Heller supervised the launch of several highly successful magazines such as *Campaign*, *Computing*, and *Accountancy Age*. His many acclaimed – and worldwide best-selling – books include *The Naked Manager*, *Culture Shock*, *The Age of the Common Millionaire*, *The Way to Win* (with Will Carling), *The Complete Guide to Modern Management*, and *In Search of European Excellence*.